Are We There Yet, Mama?

Written by Elena Castro, Barbara Flores, and Eddie Hernández
Illustrated by Mary Ramirez

Celebration Press
An Imprint of Addison-Wesley Educational Publishers, Inc.

The trip to my grandparents' house takes a long time. My mom and I go by car.

We leave El Paso, Texas, in the morning.
"Are we there yet, Mama?," I ask.
"No, dear, we have a long way to go,"
she says.

Soon we get to Las Cruces, New Mexico.
"Are we there yet, Mama?," I ask.
"No, dear, we have a long way to go,"
she says.

Soon we get to Tucson, Arizona.
"Are we there yet, Mama?," I ask.
"No, dear, we still have a long way to go," she says.

Soon we get to Los Angeles, California.
"Are we there yet, Mama?," I ask.
"No, dear, we still have a long way to go,"
she says.

10

Soon we get to Bakersfield, California.
"Are we there yet, Mama?," I ask.
"No, dear, we still have a long way to go," she says.

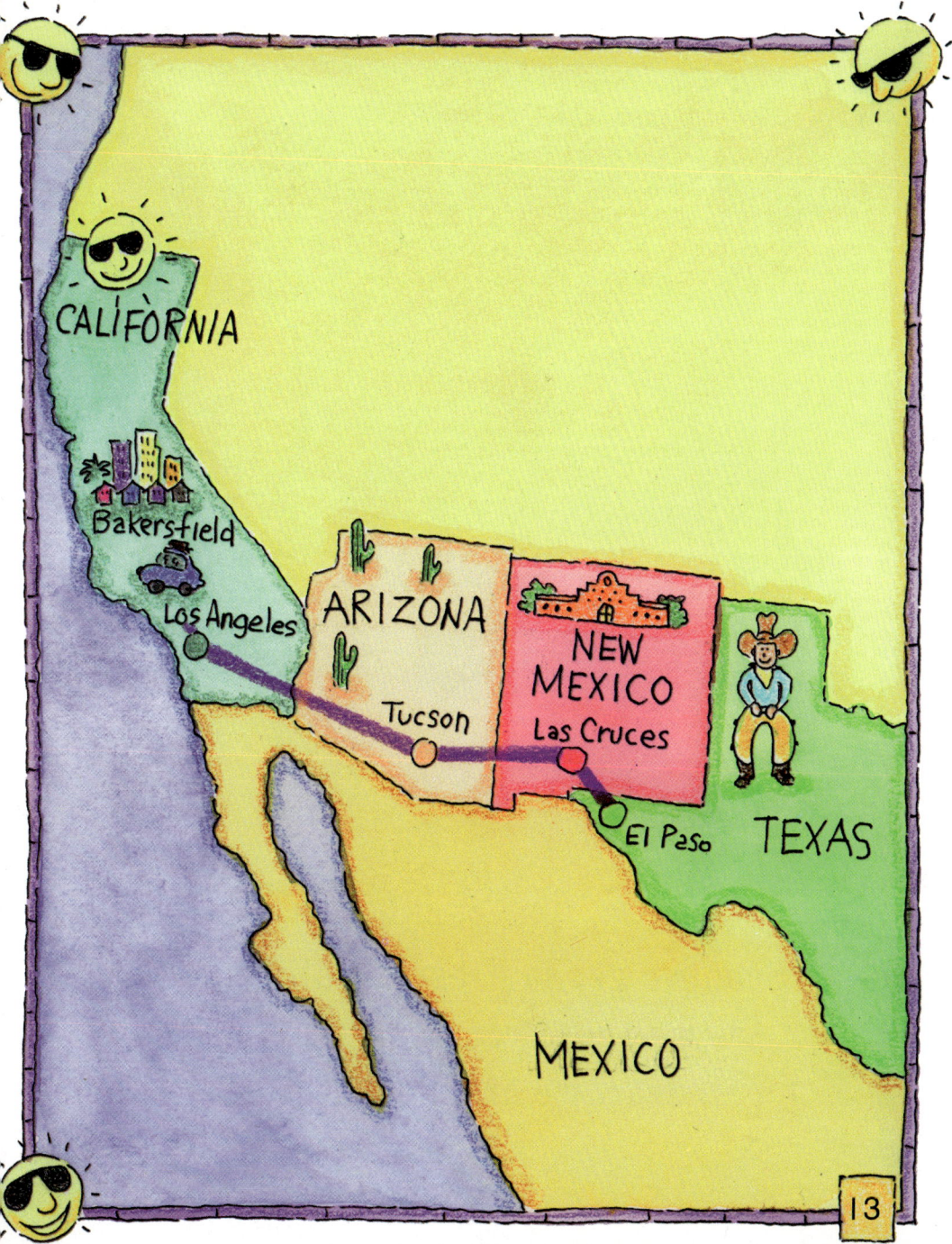

Soon we get to Fresno, California.
"Are we there yet, Mama?," I ask.
"Yes, dear, we are almost there."

Soon we get to my grandparents' house.
"Grandpa, Grandma, we're here!"